Written by Annabel Blackledge
Art editor Kate Mullins
Editorial director Louise Pritchard
Design director Jill Plank

Pangolin Books
An imprint of Bookwork Ltd

First published in the UK in 2004 by
Bookwork Ltd, Unit 17 Piccadilly Mill,
Lower Street, Stroud, Gloucestershire, GL5 2HT

Copyright © 2004 Bookwork Ltd

All rights reserved. No part of this publication may be reproduced, stored in a retrieval system, or transmitted in any form or by any other means, electronic, mechanical, photocopying, recording or otherwise, without the prior written consent of of the copyright owner.

A CIP catalogue record for this book is
available from the British Library.

ISBN 1 84493 009 2

Colour reproduction by
Black Cat Graphics Ltd, Bristol, UK
Printed in England by
Goodman Baylis Ltd

Before the introduction of **photo-finishes** for the 1932 Games, judges had to make **split-second decisions** when athletes crossed the finishing line close together.

INTRODUCTION

The first Olympic Games were held in 776 BCE in *Ancient Greece*. The games were held *every four years* until CE393, when they were banned by Emperor Theodosius I.

Frenchman Pierre de Courbertin was responsible for the *revival of the Games*. The first modern Olympics were held in Athens, Greece, in 1896.

The *Paralympic Games* are for athletes with disabilities. Ludwig Guttman pioneered the Paralympics when he organised the 1948 Wheelchair Games to coincide with the London Olympics.

The Olympic motto is *'faster, higher, stronger'* – a fitting incentive for all athletes striving to achieve great things at the world's *greatest sporting festival*.

Volleyball

Volleyball has been an Olympic sport since the Tokyo Games in 1964. ★ It was invented in the USA by William G Morgan, and was originally called Mintonette. Morgan created the game as an alternative to basketball, with less physical contact. ★ Volleyball is played indoors on a court. Two teams use their hands, arms and upper bodies to volley a ball back and forth over a high net. ★ Beach volleyball is an outdoor version of the game played on sand. It became an Olympic sport in Atlanta, USA, in 1996.

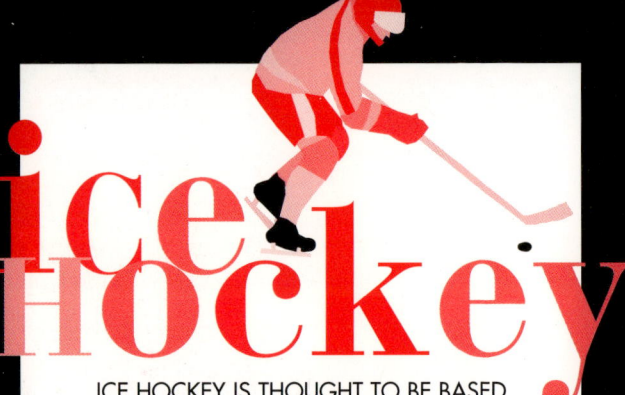

Ice Hockey

Ice hockey is thought to be based on a game played in the 1800s by **MICMAC INDIANS** in Canada. ★ The 1920 Summer Olympics **WERE THE FIRST** to include ice hockey. ★ The puck is a **RUBBER DISC** used instead of a hockey ball. It can fly across the ice at more than 150 km/hr! ★ The **SLAP SHOT** is the fastest ice hockey shot. ★ The **ZAMBONI** is a machine that resurfaces the ice during the game.

GYMNASTICS 5

Gymnastics

GYMNASTICS WAS PART OF THE EARLY OLYMPIC GAMES IN *Ancient Greece*. THE WORD GYMNASTICS COMES FROM THE GREEK WORD *GYMNOS*, MEANING *naked* – ANCIENT GREEK GYMNASTS COMPETED *in the nude!* ANCIENT OLYMPIC GYMNASTIC EVENTS INCLUDED *rope climbing* AND *club swinging*. ★ MODERN OLYMPIC GYMNASTS COMPETE ON APPARATUS LIKE THE *beam* AND THE *bars*, AND WITH *hoops, balls* AND *ribbons*. ★ IN 1976, ROMANIAN GYMNAST NADIA COMENECI BECAME THE FIRST GYMNAST TO SCORE A *perfect ten*, AT JUST 14 YEARS OF AGE.

Boxing

BOXING WAS BANNED FROM THE FIRST MODERN OLYMPICS HELD IN 1896 BECAUSE IT WAS CONSIDERED TOO DANGEROUS. IT WAS REINTRODUCED FOR A YEAR IN 1904 – THE USA WERE THE ONLY TEAM TO ENTER – AND CAME BACK FOR GOOD IN 1920. ★ ANCIENT GREEK OLYMPIC BOXERS PROTECTED THEIR FISTS WITH STRIPS OF SOFT LEATHER. ★ THE ROMANS MADE THEIR FISTS INTO DEADLY WEAPONS BY STRAPPING SPIKES TO THEIR FINGERS!

ski jumping

It is believed that ski jumping began on the snowy mountains of northern Europe as a CHILDREN'S GAME. ★ EDDIE THE EAGLE is the anti-hero of the sport. He came last in every event at the 1988 Winter Games in Calgary, Canada. ★ Olympic ski jumpers compete on two hills. The NORMAL HILL is 90m high and the LARGE HILL is 120m high. ★ Top jumpers can reach SPEEDS of up to 90km/hr and can leap DISTANCES of more than 200m.

CURLING • ARCHERY   7

Curling

CURLING IS LIKE A FORM OF **BOWLING OR DARTS ON ICE**. ★ IT WAS ORIGINALLY PLAYED ON **FROZEN PONDS AND LOCHS** IN 16TH-CENTURY SCOTLAND. ★ TEAMS OF PLAYERS TAKE TURNS TO **SLIDE** A SPECIAL STONE ACROSS THE ICE TOWARDS A **TARGET** CALLED A **HOUSE**. OTHER MEMBERS OF THE TEAM **SMOOTH THE PATH** IN FRONT OF THE STONE WITH A SPECIAL BROOM. ★ THE ICE RINK IS SPRINKLED WITH WATER BEFORE EACH GAME. THE DROPS FREEZE, MAKING THE ICE **PEBBLED**, SO REDUCING FRICTION BETWEEN IT AND THE STONE.

archery

THE EARLIEST RECORDS OF *bows and arrows* BEING USED FOR HUNTING AND WARFARE GO BACK TO *ancient Egypt*. THE FIRST KNOWN *competition* WAS HELD IN THE UK IN 1583. ★ IN OLYMPIC COMPETITIONS, ARCHERS STAND 70M AWAY FROM A 1.22M-WIDE TARGET. THE TARGET LOOKS THE SIZE OF A *drawing pin* HELD AT ARM'S LENGTH TO THE ARCHER. ★ IF AN ARCHER *splits* THE SHAFT OF AN ARROW ALREADY IN THE TARGET, IT IS REFERRED TO AS A *Robin Hood*.

8 SPEED SKATING

speed skating

This sport began in the Netherlands as a way of crossing the canals in the winter. ★ Speed skaters wear skin-tight body suits to make them more streamlined and glasses to protect their eyes from ice chips and from glare. ★ Speed skates are called clap skates. They are not fully fixed to the boot and 'clap' as the skater lifts each foot. The blades' prolonged contact with the ice increases the skater's speed. ★ In 2000, Australian skater Steve Bradbury came from last place to take the gold medal in the men's 1000m race – the other competitors fell over.

synchronised swimming

SYNCHRONISED SWIMMING IS ONE OF JUST THREE OLYMPIC EVENTS **OPEN ONLY TO WOMEN.** ★ SYNCHRONISED SWIMMING WAS MADE POPULAR BY THE AUSTRALIAN SWIMMER ANNETTE KELLERMAN, WHO TOURED THE USA IN 1907, PERFORMING WATER ACROBATICS **IN A GLASS TANK.** ★ PARTICIPANTS ARE NOT ALLOWED TO WEAR GOGGLES OR A **TRANSPARENT** SWIMMING COSTUME! ★ MOVES INCLUDE THE **ROCKET** AND THE **EGGBEATER.**

football

FOOTBALL WAS INTRODUCED AS AN OLYMPIC SPORT IN 1900. IT WAS ONE OF THE FIRST OLYMPIC TEAM SPORTS. ★ PARALYMPIC FOOTBALL MATCHES ARE PLAYED ON SMALLER PITCHES THAN OLYMPIC MATCHES. THE GOALS ARE SMALLER TOO, AND EACH TEAM HAS SEVEN RATHER THAN ELEVEN PLAYERS. ★ NOT A SINGLE PLAYER WAS SENT OFF DURING THE WOMEN'S FOOTBALL TOURNAMENT AT THE 2000 OLYMPICS HELD IN SYDNEY, AUSTRALIA. ★ DURING THE 1920 FINALS, THE CZECH TEAM WALKED OFF THE PITCH IN PROTEST AT A DECISION BY THE REFEREE. THEIR OPPONENTS, BELGIUM, WERE AWARDED GOLD.

wrestling

- Wrestling is said to be the world's OLDEST COMPETITIVE SPORT.
- Ancient wrestling was much more VIOLENT than competitions today. BITING and STRANGLING were encouraged, and some events were performed knee-deep in MUD!
- GRECO-ROMAN and FREESTYLE wrestling are part of the modern Games. Greco-Roman wrestlers fight only with their arms and upper bodies. Freestyle wrestlers are also allowed to use their legs.
- WOMEN were not allowed to take part in wrestling events until the 2004 Games in Athens, Greece.

canoeing

CANOES AND KAYAKS ARE BASED ON TRADITIONAL NATIVE AMERICAN AND INUIT BOATS USED FOR FISHING. ★ A CANOE IS OPEN AT THE TOP, AND IS PADDLED FROM A KNEELING POSITION USING A SINGLE-BLADED PADDLE. ONLY MEN COMPETE IN CANOEING EVENTS TODAY. ★ A KAYAK IS CLOSED AT THE TOP AND PADDLED FROM A SEATED POSITION USING A DOUBLE-BLADED PADDLE. ★ IN THE OLYMPICS, COMPETITORS RACE THE BOATS EITHER IN FLAT WATER OR IN WHITE WATER WHILE NEGOTIATING SLALOM OBSTACLES.

Snowboarding

Snowboarding is a modern sport. It began to develop in the 1960s and was first included in the Olympics in the winter of 1998. ★ Snowboarding is a bit like surfing, a bit like skiing and a bit like skateboarding. ★ Olympic snowboarders compete in two types of events. In the parallel giant slalom, competitors race in pairs down a steep, snowy slalom course. In the halfpipe event, snowboarders perform tricks on a U-shaped, icy course. ★ If a snowboarder bumps into anything, it is called a bonk!

diving

- DIVING BEGAN SO THAT PEOPLE COULD PRACTISE GYMNASTICS OVER WATER – A GUARANTEED SOFT LANDING! DIVING SOON BECAME POPULAR IN ITS OWN RIGHT AND HAS FEATURED AT EVERY SUMMER OLYMPICS SINCE 1908.
- A NEW DIVING EVENT – SYNCHRONISED DIVING – WAS INTRODUCED TO THE OLYMPICS IN 2000. PAIRS OF DIVERS LEAVE THE BOARD TOGETHER, AIMING TO SYNCHRONISE THEIR MOVES PERFECTLY.
- THE YOUNGEST EVER OLYMPIC GOLD MEDALIST WAS 13-YEAR-OLD FU MINGXIA FROM CHINA. SHE WON THE WOMEN'S 10M PLATFORM EVENT IN 1992.

POLO

- Polo is a game in which teams of four players try to score goals by hitting a small ball with a long mallet, all while riding a pony!
- Polo has been played at five Olympics, and its last appearance was in 1936.
- Water polo is a variation on polo that has been part of the Games since 1908. Water polo players originally rode on floating barrels using mallets to hit the ball, but they now swim and use their hands to score. Players are not allowed to touch the sides or bottom of the pool when the ball is in play.

fencing

Fencing is a type of **sword play** based on **ancient combat skills**. ★ It became a popular sport in the 17th century, when practice-weapons with **foiled**, or flattened, tips were introduced. It has been a part of every Olympic Games since 1896. ★ Wheelchair fencing was introduced to the Paralympics in 1960. The chairs are **fixed to the floor** to allow competitors **free use of their arms**. ★ Modern fencers wear a special **wired suit** connected to a central **scoring system**. The suit indicates when a hit has occurred and scores accordingly. ★ Following a disagreement at the 1924 Games in Paris, France, a **real duel** took place between the **judge** and one of the competitors. The men were separated after two hours for fear they might **bleed to death**!

14   FIGURE SKATING

figure
skating

THERE ARE FOUR EVENTS FOR FIGURE SKATERS AT THE WINTER OLYMPICS – WOMEN'S SINGLES, MEN'S SINGLES, PAIRS AND ICE DANCING. ★ ICE DANCING IS A BIT LIKE BALLROOM DANCING. COUPLES PERFORM THREE DANCES – A COMPULSORY ONE, AN ORIGINAL ONE AND A FREE ONE. THE FREE DANCE IS THE ONLY ONE WHERE SKATERS CAN CHOOSE THEIR OWN MUSIC AND MOVES. ★ THE CAMEL SPIN, THE STAR LIFT AND THE THROW JUMP ARE ALL MOVES USED BY FIGURE SKATERS.

TRAMPOLINING

The 2003 Olympic Games in Sydney, Australia, were the first to feature trampolining as part of the gymnastics programme. Russia took the gold in both the men's and the women's competitions. ★ *The word trampoline comes from the Spanish for diving board.* ★ *Trampolines have been used in training by pilots and astronauts. Practice on trampolines provided them with experience of orientation and body positions during flight.*

HURDLING

Hurdling is thought to have originated in the UK, where athletes jumped over wooden sheep gates. Hurdles have since been modernised, but the height for men's events is still the same – 0.914m. ★ *David George Burghley was known as Lord of the Hurdles. He won gold in the 400m hurdles at the 1928 Games, and was believed to be the first to practise with matchboxes balanced on his hurdles. He learned to hurdle low enough to knock the boxes off with his foot but clear the hurdle. This allowed him to run more smoothly and faster than his fellow hurdlers.*

Long Jump

Until 1908, two forms of long jump were performed at the Olympic Games. Athletes took off from a standstill in the *standing* long jump and took a run up for the *running* long jump. The run up allowed athletes to jump *much further*, and the standing long jump was abandoned after 1908. ★ The *faster* the run up, the *longer* the jump, so *sprinters* make excellent long jumpers. In 1900, US athlete Alvin Kraenzlein won the 60m dash, the 110m and 200m hurdles and the long jump. He still holds the athletics record for the most individual *gold medals* won at a single Games.

Badminton

Badminton began in 5th-century China as *Ti Jian Zi* – with a shuttlecock, but no rackets. Players KICKED THE SHUTTLECOCK to and fro! ★ Rackets known as BATTLEDORES were introduced in the 1600s, and badminton soon became popular with members of the UPPER CLASSES in the UK. ★ Badminton is the WORLD'S FASTEST RACKET SPORT. It requires LIGHTENING FAST REACTIONS. ★ A flick is a TRICK SHOT. Players try to take their opponents by surprise by using a quick FLICK OF THE WRIST to turn a slow, soft shot into a much faster one.

BOBSLEIGH

Bobsleigh, developed on the snowy slopes of Switzerland by tourists in the late 1800s, is an extreme form of tobogganing. Bobsleighs can travel at more than 135km/hr, and the team can be subjected to five times the force of gravity. Bobsleigh has been part of the Olympics since the first Winter Games in 1924.

Sailing has been a means of transport for hundreds of years, but probably originated AS A SPORT in the Netherlands. It was brought to England in the 1600s by CHARLES II. ★ Sailing is the only Olympic sport in history that has had its name changed. It first entered the programme in 1900 as YACHTING, made its next appearance in 1908 and has featured at every Games since. The sport wasn't referred to as sailing until the 2000 Games in Sydney, Australia. ★ Women originally TEAMED UP with men in Olympic sailing events, but in 1986, separate events were introduced EXCLUSIVELY for women.

✪ IN THE POLE VAULT, ATHLETES PROPEL THEMSELVES OVER A HIGH BAR USING A LONG, CARBON FIBRE POLE. BUT THE SPORT ORIGINATED IN THE UK AS A WAY OF CROSSING WATER CHANNELS – THE LENGTH OF THE VAULT WAS FAR MORE IMPORTANT THAN THE HEIGHT!

✪ POLES WERE ORIGINALLY MADE FROM BAMBOO – THE RECORD VAULT WAS JUST OVER 3M. WITH HI-TECH MODERN POLES, SOME TOP ATHLETES CAN VAULT OVER BARS SET AT 6M.

✪ REVEREND BOB RICHARDS WAS KNOWN AS THE VAULTING VICAR. HE IS THE ONLY POLE VAULTER TO HAVE WON GOLD TWICE – ONCE IN 1952 AND AGAIN IN 1956.

EVENTING 19

eventing

Eventing is made up of three riding disciplines – *dressage, show jumping* and *cross country*. ★ Olympic equestrian events were originally open only to men in the *armed forces*. This restriction was lifted in 1952, when women were also permitted to take part for the first time. ★ Eventing is the *ultimate team sport*, with horse and rider working together in *perfect unison*. ★ Eventing is one of the few Olympic sports in which *men and women* compete with and against each other *on equal terms*.

pentathlon

THE MODERN PENTATHLON CONSISTS OF FIVE DIFFERENT EVENTS – RIDING, FENCING, SHOOTING, RUNNING AND SWIMMING. ★ LEGEND HAS IT THAT THE EVENTS – ORIGINALLY CALLED THE MILITARY PENTATHLON – ARE BASED ON THE ADVENTURES OF A 19TH-CENTURY FRENCH CAVALRY SOLDIER. THE SOLDIER WAS SENT INTO ENEMY TERRITORY TO DELIVER A MESSAGE. HE RODE OVER ROUGH GROUND UNTIL HE WAS CONFRONTED AND CHALLENGED TO A SWORD FIGHT. THE SOLDIER WON THE DUEL, BUT HIS HORSE WAS KILLED BY AN ENEMY SOLDIER. THE FRENCH SOLDIER SHOT THE ENEMY AND CONTINUED ON FOOT, SWAM ACROSS A RIVER AND FINALLY DELIVERED THE MESSAGE. ★ THE PENTATHLON WAS ORIGINALLY INTRODUCED TO THE OLYMPICS AS A WAY OF DETERMINING THE GREATEST ALL-ROUND ATHLETE.

HIGH JUMP

GERMAN HIGH JUMPER GERD WESSIG IS OVER 2M TALL – A HUGE ADVANTAGE IN THIS EVENT! IN 1980, HE BECAME THE ONLY HIGH JUMPER EVER TO SET A WORLD RECORD AT THE OLYMPICS. ★ THE FOSBURY FLOP – A BACKWARD FLIP OVER THE BAR – IS THE MOST POPULAR STYLE OF HIGH JUMP TODAY. JUDGES COULDN'T BELIEVE THEIR EYES WHEN DICK FOSBURY INTRODUCED HIS REVOLUTIONARY TECHNIQUE AT THE 1968 GAMES. ★ THE 1952 RUSSIAN OLYMPIC HIGH JUMP TEAM WORE SPECIAL HIGH-SOLED SHOES – THIS DUBIOUS TACTIC WAS LATER BANNED!

Shooting

SHOOTING EVENTS HAVE BEEN PART OF THE OLYMPIC GAMES *on and off* SINCE 1896. ★ AT THE 1968 GAMES IN MEXICO, *women* COMPETED FOR THE FIRST TIME, IN *mixed events* ALONGSIDE THE MEN. WOMEN'S EVENTS WERE NOT TOTALLY SEPARATED FROM THE MEN'S UNTIL 1996. ★ SWEDISH SHOOTER OSCAR SWAHN WAS THE *oldest ever Olympian*. HE WON HIS FIRST GOLD MEDAL IN 1908 AT THE AGE OF 60 AND WON A SILVER MEDAL WHEN HE WAS 72. ★ HUNGARY'S KAROLY TAKACS HAD TO LEARN TO SHOOT LEFT-HANDED AFTER A CLOSE ENCOUNTER WITH A WWII *hand grenade* IN 1938. HE WENT ON TO WIN *two gold medals*.

luge

Luge is one of the MOST DANGEROUS Olympic sports. Competitors lie on their back on a tiny sled and RACE down an ICY track at SPEEDS of as much as 140km/hr! ★ *Olympic luge champion Georg Hackl CAUSED A STIR at the 1998 Winter Games when he competed in a pair of bright yellow SUPER BOOTS! He claimed that the aerodynamic boots helped him to win his THIRD GOLD medal.*

Marathon

THE FIRST OLYMPIC MARATHON WAS RUN IN 1896 BETWEEN THE GREEK CITIES OF MARATHON AND ATHENS – A DISTANCE OF 42KM. ★ AT THE LONDON OLYMPICS IN 1908, THE MARATHON WAS MADE 195M LONGER SO THAT MEMBERS OF THE BRITISH ROYAL FAMILY COULD WATCH THE RACE FROM THE COMFORT OF WINDSOR CASTLE. 42KM AND 195M LATER BECAME THE OFFICIAL LENGTH OF THE MARATHON. ★ US ATHLETE FRED LORZ WAS DISQUALIFIED FROM THE 1904 OLYMPIC MARATHON WHEN IT WAS REVEALED THAT HE HAD TRAVELLED PART OF THE COURSE IN A CAR!

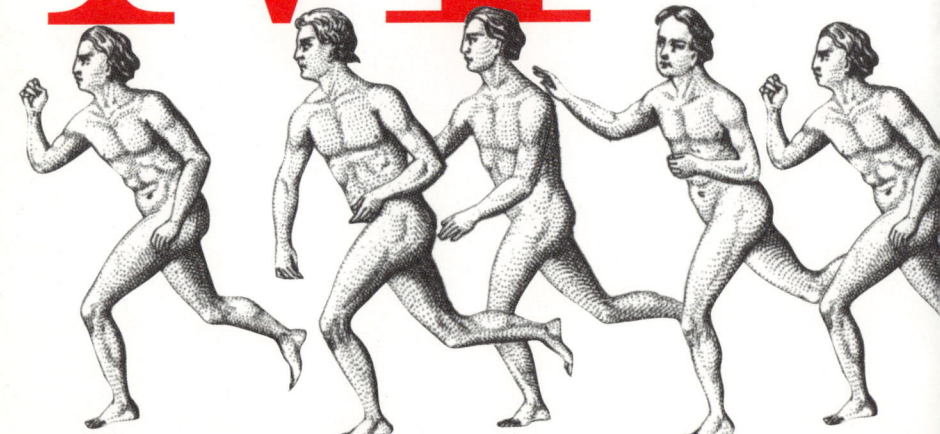

ROWING

Rowing has been part of the modern Olympics every year except for 1896 in Athens, when the SEA WAS TOO STORMY for the races to go ahead. ★ *Rowers average more than 40 strokes per minute – a true TEST OF ENDURANCE.* ★ *Olympic champion Steve Redgrave is known as the ATHLETE OF THE CENTURY. He won five Olympic golds between 1984 and 2000.* ★ *If a rower makes a faulty stroke, it is called CATCHING A CRAB.*

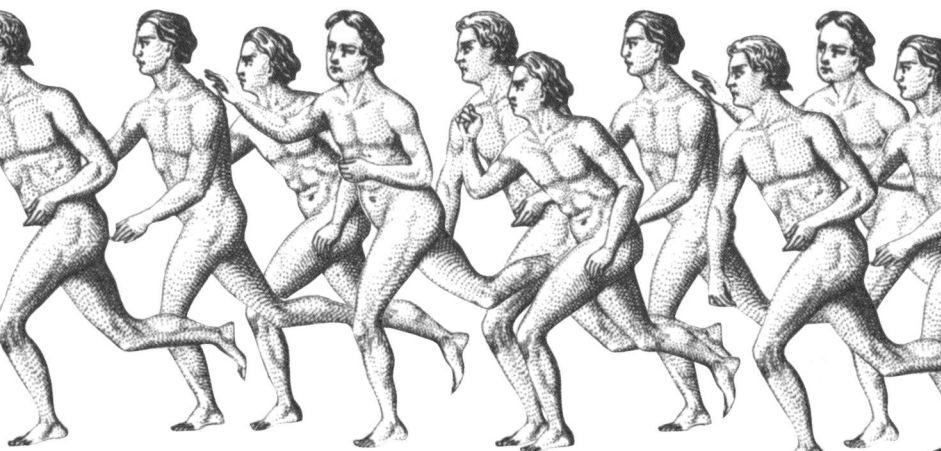

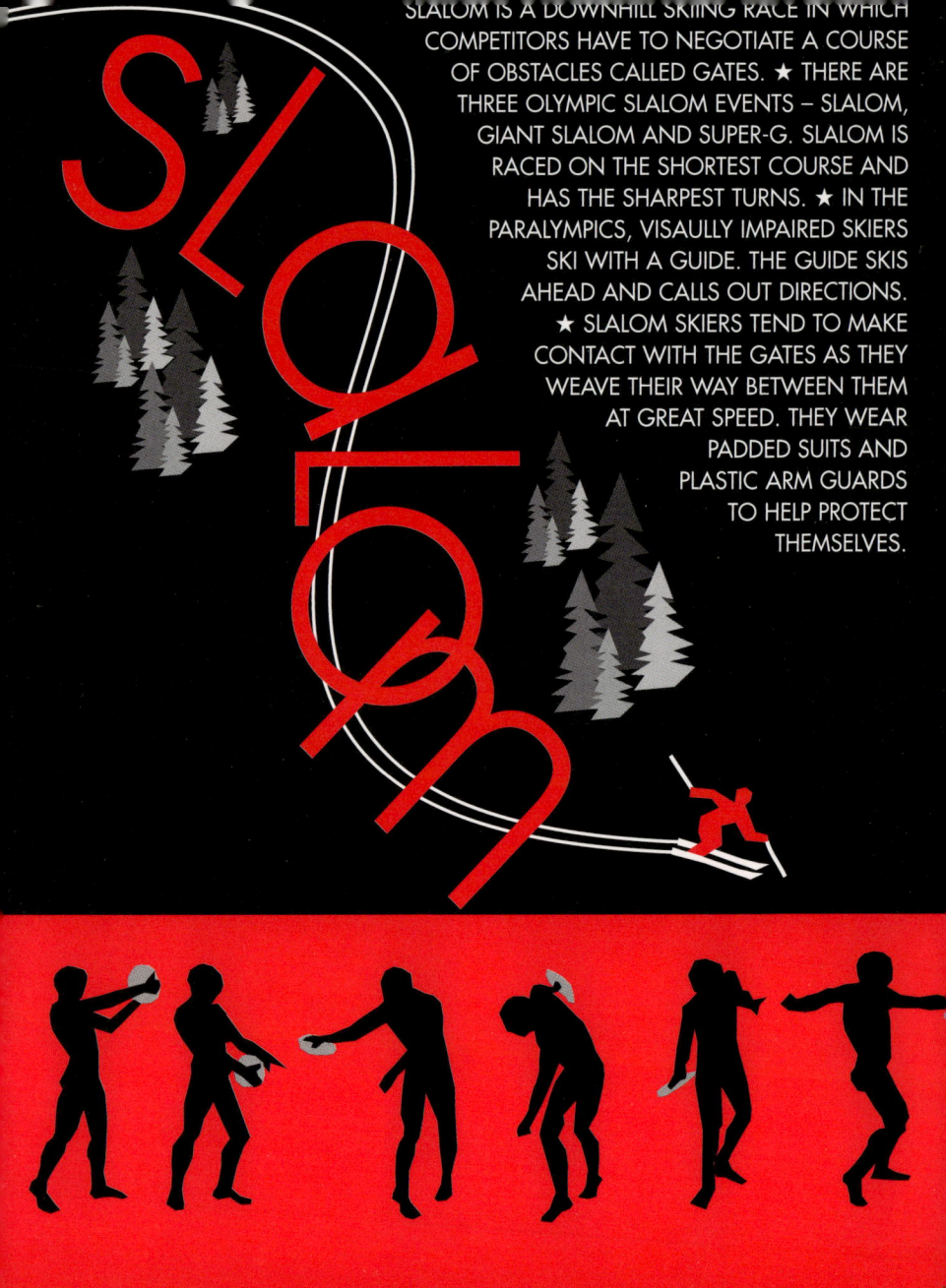

SLALOM

SLALOM IS A DOWNHILL SKIING RACE IN WHICH COMPETITORS HAVE TO NEGOTIATE A COURSE OF OBSTACLES CALLED GATES. ★ THERE ARE THREE OLYMPIC SLALOM EVENTS – SLALOM, GIANT SLALOM AND SUPER-G. SLALOM IS RACED ON THE SHORTEST COURSE AND HAS THE SHARPEST TURNS. ★ IN THE PARALYMPICS, VISAULLY IMPAIRED SKIERS SKI WITH A GUIDE. THE GUIDE SKIS AHEAD AND CALLS OUT DIRECTIONS. ★ SLALOM SKIERS TEND TO MAKE CONTACT WITH THE GATES AS THEY WEAVE THEIR WAY BETWEEN THEM AT GREAT SPEED. THEY WEAR PADDED SUITS AND PLASTIC ARM GUARDS TO HELP PROTECT THEMSELVES.

SWIMMING

Hungarian Alfred Hajos won the gold medal in the first modern Olympics swimming event in Athens, Greece, in 1896. Competitors were taken *out to sea* in a boat, and they swam back to shore! ★ *Eric the Eel*, Eric Moussambani from Equatorial Guinea, learned to swim just nine months before the 2000 Games in Sydney. He won his heat and qualified for the next round of the men's 100m freestyle event, despite never before swimming 100m *without stopping*. It took Eric nearly 2 minutes to complete the race, but his opponents were disqualified! ★ French Paralympian Beatrice Hess swam her way to seven *gold medals* at the Sydney 2000 Games and *smashed* several *world records*.

Discus

Discus was on the programme at the ancient Olympics, and the event has barely changed since then – although modern competitors wear more clothes! ★ Discus originally made up part of the ancient pentathlon, along with running, jumping, javelin and wrestling. ★ US athlete Alfred Oerter is considered to be the greatest discus thrower of modern times. He won the Olympic gold medal four times in a row – in 1956, 1960, 1964 and 1968.

Cycling events have appeared at EVERY OLYMPICS since 1896, and over the years racing bicycles have CHANGED MORE than any other Olympic sports equipment. ★ The bikes used in 1896 were UNCOMFORTABLE to ride, heavy and RATHER SLOW. The race took place on the same course as the marathon. ★ Modern TRACK RACING bicycles are LIGHTWEIGHT and are usually made from carbon fibre, aluminium and titanium. The semi-solid wheels and tilted position of the rider make the bikes EXTREMELY AERODYNAMIC.

cycling

shot put

A SHOT IS A METAL BALL THAT WEIGHS 7.26KG IN MEN'S EVENTS AND 4KG IN WOMEN'S EVENTS. IT IS CALLED A SHOT BECAUSE IT RESEMBLES A CANNON SHOT, OR BALL. ★ US POLICEMAN PATRICK MCDONALD WON A GOLD MEDAL FOR SHOT PUT IN 1912 AGED 42. HE REMAINS THE OLDEST PERSON EVER TO WIN AN OLYMPIC GOLD IN ATHLETICS. ★ SHOT PUT BECAME SO POPULAR IN THE UK DURING THE 1300S THAT KING EDWARD III BANNED IT. HE FEARED THAT MEN WERE PUTTING THE SHOT INSTEAD OF PRACTISING THEIR ARCHERY!

TENNIS • TORCH 27

Tennis

The earliest form of tennis was called *jeu de paume*, which is French for 'palm game'. It was played on a walled court using the palm of the hand instead of a racket. ★ John Boland travelled from Ireland to the 1896 Games in Athens, Greece, as a spectator ... and came home with a gold medal! His friend had entered him for the tennis, and he won, despite having to play in his everyday shoes! ★ German tennis ace Steffi Graf won the ladies' Olympic tennis demonstration singles in 1984 at the age of just 15.

Torch

The ancient Greek Olympics were held to honour the god Zeus – a flame burned at his altar throughout the Games. Competitors also took part in a naked relay, passing a flaming torch instead of a baton and receiving encouraging slaps from the audience as they ran! ★ The flame returned to the Games in 1928. A torch has been carried in a relay from the site of the ancient Games to the host city since 1936.

athletics

Modern Olympic athletics includes all *track, field, road* and *combined* events, and has been part of the Games since ancient times. ★ Jesse Owens was the *hero* of the 1936 Berlin Games. He *won gold* in the 100m, 200m, long jump and 4x100m relay. ★ UK wheelchair athlete Tanni Grey-Thompson is a champion of various events, from 100m *sprints* to *marathons*. She has won a *grand total* of *13 medals* at the Paralympic Games, and was awarded an *OBE* in the Millennium New Year's Honours list.

Basketball

Basketball was invented in the USA in 1891 as a way for students to KEEP FIT indoors during the COLD winter months. ★ The game was originally played with FOOTBALLS and FRUIT BASKETS nailed to the gymnasium wall. A helper ON A LADDER had to be on hand to pick the football from the baskets. ★ The USA put forward an ALL-STAR basketball team for the 1992 Barcelona Olympic Games. MICHAEL JORDAN, MAGIK JOHNSON and LARRY BIRD won their country a GOLD MEDAL and were dubbed THE DREAM TEAM for their brilliant performance. ★ An AIRBALL is a shot that misses the net altogether. ★ A DUNK is a basket scored by slamming the ball down into the net with one or both hands.

tug-of-war

THE FIRST EVIDENCE OF TUG-OF-WAR COMES FROM AN ANCIENT EGYPTIAN TOMB PAINTING DATING FROM ABOUT 2500BCE. IT APPEARS THAT THE EGYPTIANS DID NOT TUG ON A ROPE, BUT LINKED ARMS AND TRIED TO PULL THE OTHER TEAM OVER A LINE ON THE GROUND. ★ TUG-OF-WAR APPEARED ON THE OLYMPIC GAMES PROGRAMME JUST SIX TIMES, BETWEEN 1900 AND 1920. ★ A TUG-OF-WAR CONTEST WAS FEATURED ON A COMMEMORATIVE COIN FOR THE 1988 GAMES HELD IN SEOUL, KOREA. ★ THE CITY OF LONDON POLICE TEAM ARE STILL THE REIGNING TUG-OF-WAR OLYMPIC CHAMPIONS. THEY WON GOLD FOR THE UK IN 1908 AND AGAIN IN 1920 – THE LAST TIME TUG-OF-WAR WAS FEATURED AT THE GAMES.

Javelin

Javelin has been an Olympic event since ancient times, but the sport has changed *over the centuries*. In ancient Greece, javelins were *thrown at targets*. It wasn't until the 19th century that javelins were thrown for *distance* only, and the modern version of the sport developed. ★ Ancient Olympians had a secret weapon to help them throw further. It was a leather thong called an *amentum* wound round the javelin to make it *spin in the air* and travel much further. The amentum was later *banned* because it was considered *dangerous*!

GAMES CALENDAR

Cities that wish to host the Summer (S) or Winter (W) Games must first apply to the International Olympic Committee (IOC). The potential of the applicants is assessed, some are accepted as candidates and the host is eventually elected by members of the IOC. The Summer and Winter Olympics are now held alternately every two years. The Paralympic Games take place in the same city and year as the Olympics.

- Athens, Greece – 1896 (S)
- Paris, France – 1900 (S)
- St Louis, USA – 1904 (S)
- London, UK – 1908 (S)
- Stockholm, Sweden – 1912 (S)
- 1916 Games cancelled because of WWI
- Antwerp, Belgium – 1920 (S)
- Chamonix, France – 1924 (W)
- Paris, France – 1924 (S)
- St Moritz, Switzerland – 1928 (W)
- Amsterdam, Holland – 1928 (S)
- Lake Placid, USA – 1932 (W)
- Los Angeles, USA – 1932 (S)
- Garmisch-Partenkirchen, Germany – 1936 (W)
- Berlin, Germany – 1936 (S)
- 1940 and 1944 Games cancelled because of WWII
- St Moritz, Switzerland – 1948 (W)
- London, UK – 1948 (S)
- Oslo, Norway – 1952 (W)
- Helsinki, Finland – 1952 (S)
- Cortina d'Ampezzo, Italy – 1956 (W)
- Melbourne, Australia – 1956 (S)
- Squaw Valley, USA – 1960 (W)
- Rome, Italy – 1960 (S)
- Innsbruck, Austria – 1964 (W)
- Tokyo, Japan – 1964 (S)
- Grenoble, France – 1968 (W)
- Mexico City, Mexico – 1968 (S)
- Sapporo, Japan – 1972 (W)
- Munich, Germany – 1972 (S)
- Innsbruck, Austria – 1976 (W)
- Montreal, Canada – 1976 (S)
- Lake Placid, USA – 1980 (W)
- Moscow, USSR – 1980 (S)
- Sarajevo, Yugoslavia – 1984 (W)
- Los Angeles, USA – 1984 (S)
- Calgary, Canada – 1988 (W)
- Seoul, Korea – 1988 (S)
- Albertville, France – 1992 (W)
- Barcelona, Spain – 1992 (S)
- Lillehammer, Norway – 1994 (W)
- Atlanta, USA – 1996 (S)
- Nagano, Japan – 1998 (W)
- Sydney, Australia – 2000 (S)
- Salt Lake City, USA – 2002 (W)
- Athens, Greece – 2004 (S)
- Torino, Italy – 2006 (W)
- Beijing, China – 2008 (S)
- Vancouver, Canada – 2010 (W)

INDEX

AB
ARCHERY 7, 26
ATHLETICS 26, 28
BADMINTON 16
BASKETBALL 4, 29
BIRD LARRY 29
BOBSLEIGH 17
BOLAND, JOHN 27
BOXING 6
BRADBURY, STEVE 8
BURGHLEY, DAVID GEORGE 15

CD
CANOEING 10
COMENECI, NADIA 5
CURLING 7
CYCLING 26
DISCUS 25
DIVING 12, 15

EFG
EAGLE, EDDIE THE 6
EEL, ERIC THE 25
EVENTING 19
FENCING 13, 20
FIGURE SKATING 14
FOOTBALL 9, 29
FOSBURY, DICK 21
GRAF, STEFFI 27
GREY-THOMPSON, TANNI 28
GYMNASTICS 5, 12, 15

HIJK
HACKL, GEORG 22
HAJOS, ALFRED 25
HESS, BEATRICE 25
HIGH JUMP 21
HURDLING 15
ICE HOCKEY 4
JAVELIN 25, 30
JOHNSON, MAGIK 29
JORDAN, MICHAEL 29
KAYAKING 10
KELLERMAN, ANNETTE 9
KRAENZLEIN, ALVIN 16

LMOP
LONG JUMP 16
LORZ, FRED 22
LUGE 22
MARATHON 22, 26
MINGXIA, FU 12
OERTER, ALFRED 25
OWENS, JESSE 28
PARALYMPICS 3, 9, 13, 24, 25, 28, 31
PENTATHLON 20, 25
POLE VAULT 18
POLO 12

RST
REDGRAVE, STEVE 23
RICHARDS, BOB 18
RIDING 12, 19, 20
ROWING 23
SAILING 18
SHOOTING 20, 21
SHOT PUT 26
SKI JUMPING 6
SKIING 11, 24
SLALOM 10, 11, 24
SNOWBOARDING 11
SPEED SKATING 8
SPRINTING 16, 28
SWAHN, OSCAR 21
SWIMMING 20, 25
SYNCHRONISED SWIMMING 9
TAKACS, KAROLY 21
TENNIS 27
TORCH 27
TRAMPOLINING 15
TUG-OF-WAR 29

VWY
VOLLEYBALL 4
WATER POLO 12
WESSIG, GERD 21
WRESTLING 10, 25
YACHTING 18

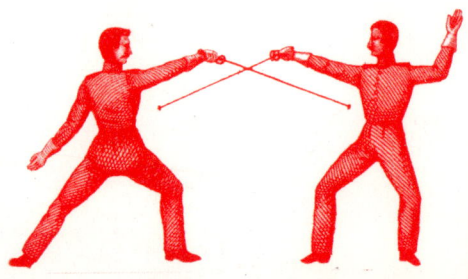

Olympic **FENCING** bouts take place on a platform called a **PISTE**. It is 1.5m wide and 14m long.